Original title:
Jupiter Jingles

Copyright © 2025 Creative Arts Management OÜ
All rights reserved.

Author: Arabella Whitmore
ISBN HARDBACK: 978-1-80567-766-6
ISBN PAPERBACK: 978-1-80567-887-8

Rhythms in the Night Sky

Stars are dancing, what a sight,
Comets winking with delight.
Planets giggle in their flight,
While moons are throwing a moonlit night.

Wobbling asteroids in a line,
Swinging low like a roller dine.
Galaxies swirl, what a design,
In this cosmic party, have some wine!

Whispering Winds of the Baron

Under clouds, the breezes chuckle,
Tickling trees with a subtle shuffle.
Rusty raindrops start to snuggle,
As starlight weaves a joyful hustle.

The baron laughs with a twinkling eye,
Riding breezes, oh so spry.
Moonbeams join, they can't deny,
Spreading giggles under the sky.

Cosmic Chimes

Planetary bells start to sing,
Echoing folly in a cosmic ring.
With each note, galaxies swing,
Creating laughter in everything.

Asteroid choirs, oh what a band,
Playing tunes across the land.
Gravity's pull, a comedic hand,
Dancing elements, ever so grand.

Echoes of the Great Red Spot

In whirlpools of color, a game is spun,
Where the storms shout jokes and have their fun.
Spots of red, under stars, they run,
Chasing halos 'til the day is done.

Each chuckle rumbles from the void,
A cosmic symphony, never destroyed.
In every twist, we find joy,
With laughter in space, no one's annoyed.

Beneath the Bands of Color

In a swirl of hues and glee,
Dancing storms, you can't see!
Planets play hide and seek,
With a giggle and a squeak.

Bouncing moons in a game,
Each one has its own name.
Ticklish clouds swirl around,
As laughter is found abound.

A giant's smile lights the way,
Brightening the night and day.
Stars wear hats, what a sight,
Making every dream take flight.

Rings of Resounding Joy

Round and round in perfect cheer,
Echoes of laughter we hear.
Rings of joy, spin and twirl,
Creating giggles in a whirl.

A comet joins in the fun,
Chasing beams of the sun.
With a boisterous flash and dash,
They paint the night with a splash.

Twinkling lights in a boundless space,
All are welcome in this place.
A cosmic circus, bright and loud,
In a silly, starry crowd.

The Enchanting Jovian Waltz

A dance on clouds, soft and light,
Spinning in the velvet night.
With a tickle and a tease,
It's a party of cosmic breeze!

Whirling orbs and moons that jest,
Each step a bubbling quest.
Galactic giggles—what a blast,
In a twirl that's unsurpassed!

Laughter floats on starlit wings,
As every planet joyfully sings.
Rhythms echo through the space,
A merry dance in this vast place.

Lullabies from the Sky

In the silence of the night,
Stars whisper, soft and bright.
Gentle hums from faraway,
Lullabies that sway and play.

Clouds drift by, like dreams afloat,
Cozy tales, a joyful note.
Shooting stars with playful charms,
Wrap the night in gentle arms.

With a chuckle from the moon,
Each bright laugh a lovely tune.
In a sleepy, swirling sigh,
Dreamers find their joy up high.

Starlit Symphony

In the night sky, they play,
Giggles and laughs on display.
Planets whirl and twirl around,
Silly sounds in space are found.

Shooting stars drop with a wink,
Cosmic clowns nod in sync.
Puppets made of gas and light,
Dance and jive, what a sight!

Lullabies from the Gas Giant

Sleepy clouds hum a tune,
Under the bright, smiling moon.
Bubbly storms softly sigh,
As twirling lights play nearby.

Nibbling comets bring a treat,
With sparkling crumbs, oh so sweet.
Giggling moons in a row,
Whisper dreams, soft and slow.

Radiant Dance of the Orbs

Planets spin in a merry spree,
Round and round with glee, oh whee!
Saturn's rings, like jump ropes fly,
While dodging asteroids passing by.

Funny faces on each sphere,
Chasing tails of laughter here.
A cosmic conga line we see,
Twinkling lights, pure jubilee.

Harmonies Among the Clouds

In fluffy realms of bright delight,
Clouds join hands and sway at night.
A symphony of giggles bright,
Echoes through the starry sight.

Wobbling giants, they take flight,
Making music, oh what a sight!
With jolly tunes they serenade,
Spinning joy in a cosmic parade.

Celestial Flare

In the sky with a wink, they play,
Planets bounce in a silly ballet.
Saturn's rings spin like a hula hoop,
While Mars joins in with a tiny whoop.

A comet slips on ice, what a sight!
Stars giggle like kids, pure delight.
Venus twirls in a fuchsia swirl,
While the asteroids dance and twirl.

Cosmic Fables

Once a star sprouted a goofy nose,
Telling tales wherever it goes.
Nebulas burst into fits of glee,
Laughing at moons perched on a tree.

A rogue planet tried to steal the show,
But asteroid friends said, "Whoa, whoa, whoa!"
With a wink and a twist, they sabotaged,
Creating a scene that seemed so staged.

Dance of the Orbs

Galaxies twist in a lively waltz,
Dodging stars that spin, driving all a pulse.
Mercury hops and Mercury skips,
With a laugh, he gives the sun some quips.

Neptune drags along, feeling quite blue,
While the others giggle, "What's wrong with you?"
Uranus cracks jokes, a cosmic clown,
As the sun rolls its rays, never a frown.

Whirling Harmonies

In a whirlpool of laughter, they spin around,
Eclipses and laughter, a joyous sound.
Planets harmonize in a cosmic song,
Singing along to where they belong.

Shooting stars dive in a dizzying arc,
Comets with sparkles, leaving a mark.
As the galaxies giggle, all blend together,
Creating a laughter, light as a feather.

Cosmic Harmonization

In a galaxy far, a dance took flight,
Planets spin with laughter, oh what a sight.
Stars play hopscotch, skip and squeal,
Comets toss confetti, that's the deal.

Moons are juggling, full of glee,
Rings of Saturn laugh, "Look at me!"
Asteroids march in a silly parade,
While black holes giggle and attempt to evade.

Galactic puppies chase bright beams,
Shooting stars burst with sparkly dreams.
Meteor showers bring forth their cheers,
As space dust tickles, dissolving fears.

Through cosmic corridors, let joy rise,
With all the chuckles under starlit skies.
A symphony of fun, no room for frowns,
In this orchestra of joyful crowns.

Notes from the Nebula

Wobbling clouds of colors so bright,
Three-headed aliens sing with delight.
Their giggles echo through the vast expanse,
As planets twirl in a cosmic dance.

Shooting stars drop candy from the sky,
While playful asteroids loop and fly.
Comets whistle tunes of light and cheer,
Bouncing off stardust, music we hear.

A chorus of craters adds to the fun,
Creating harmonies for everyone.
As space-time swirls, a quirky tune plays,
Galactic laughter fills all the rays.

In the heart of the nebula, joy does bloom,
With every note, dispelling the gloom.
Sing along with the cosmic breeze,
And join this party whenever you please.

Celestial Revelry

At dawn of a planet, merriment wakes,
Balloons made of stars, oh what fun it makes!
Uranus winks, a jester in flight,
While Venus giggles, glowing so bright.

Little green comets juggle in pairs,
Popcorn from asteroids fills up the airs.
With laughter erupting like solar flares,
And disco balls hanging from cosmic lairs.

Gravity's game, a spin and a twirl,
As Saturn's rings shimmer and swirl.
Dancing in orbit, they find their groove,
While celestial creatures join in the move.

So gather your friends in this vast expanse,
Join the celebration, don't miss the chance!
In this cosmic carnival, hilarity reigns,
With joy and humor riding the lanes.

Orbiting Oodles of Sound

In the cosmic realm, silly tunes arise,
As planets vibrate with laughter and sighs.
Moonbeams tap dance, making time rhyme,
While black holes hum a timeless chime.

Asteroid bands play rock from afar,
With giggling meteors strumming guitars.
Neptune bounces to the beat and sway,
Encouraging laughter to fill up the day.

Pulsars blink out electric beats,
While stardust shimmies on galactic streets.
The rhythm of space, pulsating and free,
Echoing joy in infinity.

So tune in your heart to the cosmic sound,
In this universe where fun is unbound.
Join in the party as we spin 'round and 'round,
For oodles of laughter in every sound.

Spheres in Symphonic Silence

In the night where planets play,
Moons wiggle in bright ballet,
Each twirl brings a cosmic cheer,
Stars blink out their jokes so clear.

Gravity pulls with a giggle,
Comets race, and starlings wiggle,
Galactic tunes, a quirky vibe,
Space whispers tales of joy, not bribe.

Bubbles float in the cosmic sea,
A nebula shapes the laugh of glee,
Twinkling lights, a playful tease,
Orbiting jesters, feel the breeze.

Oh, the sun has lost its hat,
Mercury's cartwheeling, how about that?
Laughing stars in their bright gowns,
Outrageous fun with the cosmic clowns.

Celestial Echoes

Planets laugh in a swirling dance,
Stars exchange their merry glance,
Galaxies whirl in a wild array,
Echoes of fun light the Milky Way.

A comet trips on its shiny tail,
While meteors spin, they sing a tale,
Celestial whispers of giggly sights,
As suns burst forth with fiery lights.

Laughter echoes through cosmic tides,
Cosmic jesters tease the astral rides,
Moonbeams giggle, and stars will chime,
In the vastness, all's feeling prime.

Shooting stars toss out their puns,
Uranus spins while Saturn runs,
A universal jest, a grand accord,
In this vast sky, we're never bored.

Dancing Auroras

Auroras swirl in colors bright,
Dancing to the rhythm of the night,
With twinkling eyes and giddy twirls,
They play tag with the universe's pearls.

Underneath the cosmic scene,
Stars misplaced, yet serene,
Galactic parties in vibrant hues,
Creating laughter beneath the blues.

Beneath the moon, comets display,
Silly stunts in a grand ballet,
Whirling lights, a cosmic show,
Blasting mirth with each bright glow.

Twinkling giggles in every flash,
A universe dressed in festive dash,
In a turn of fate, the stars unite,
For a dance of joy, so pure, so light.

Celestial Mirth

In a realm where laughter sings,
Galaxies share their funny things,
Each star a jester, full of glee,
Creating joy from A to Z.

Planets toss their hats in play,
Poking fun in their own way,
Witty tails and cheeky grins,
They spin tales where fun begins.

Cosmic pranks in the twilight spread,
With shooting stars, the jokes are fed,
Orbits twirl in a dizzy chase,
Mirthful shenanigans in space.

Supernova bursts with a resounding laugh,
As stars in lines do their silly half,
Floating tales through the skies so vast,
At celestial jesters, we'll forever cast.

Symphony of the Stripes

In a band of colors bright,
Zany tunes take flight.
Red and yellow twist and sway,
Making clouds play all day.

A bouncing beat from gas so grand,
Tickling rings with a gentle hand.
Laughter echoes in the breeze,
As storms join in with ease.

Who knew the gas giants like to laugh,
While swirling in their cosmic path?
They dance and spin, oh what a view,
In this funny world, so vast and new.

Jovian Rhythms

With a bop and a roll, they groove,
A motley crew in cosmic move.
Swinging moons, they form a band,
A galactic joke, so grand!

Hold your sides, don't let them burst,
As lightning strikes and stars rehearse.
Each twist and turn, a punchline scored,
The universe laughs, never bored.

Funky gas clouds dance in waltz,
Spinning tales in cosmic vaults.
A jester's hat adorned so fine,
In this vastness, where mirth does shine.

Celestial Dance of the Giants

Spinning giants in a cosmic ball,
With giggles that can be heard by all.
Twinkling lights, they skip and hop,
With belly laughs that never stop.

Gravity pulls, but they don't care,
Each swirl and twist, a playful dare.
Hula hoops of rings and dust,
Together they swirl, they must!

A comet flies, they share a grin,
As galaxies laugh, they spin and spin.
In this frolic, there's naught to fear,
Just loving chaos, crystal clear.

Whispers from the Cosmos

A gentle chuckle in the night,
Stars giggle softly, oh so light.
Planets whisper secrets near,
In a language that we hold dear.

Dancing shadows, shining bright,
Celestial jokes in shimmering light.
They tease the moons, don't take a pause,
With cosmic puns, they hold applause.

Wobbling in their merry chase,
Time bends in this enchanted space.
As comets trail in playful glee,
What a delightful sight to see!

Chime of Distant Worlds

In the silence of the night,
A comet danced, oh what a sight!
Stars giggled in the cosmic play,
While planets bumped in disarray.

With a wink and quirky grin,
Asteroids joined the silly spin.
Moons rolled over, laughing loud,
In the glow of the galactic crowd.

Flux of the Celestial

A nebula wore a silly hat,
Spinning round like a dizzy cat.
Galaxy whirlwinds tickled stars,
Filling space with cosmic jars.

Distant suns winked with delight,
As cosmic dust took off in flight.
A black hole joked, 'Come take a dive!',
In this dance, all were alive.

Tides of the Tailored Cosmos

Rings of Saturn spun like tops,
While cosmic seas began their flops.
Galactic jokes flew far and wide,
As comets zipped with humor-tide.

Stars played tag in velvet skies,
Whispering secrets and silly lies.
In this vast and twinkling sea,
Laughter echoed endlessly.

Enchanted Atmospheres

Clouds of gas wore rainbow hues,
While galaxies shared their funny views.
Planets giggled, rolled with cheer,
Among the stars, there's no fear.

In this enchanted, wacky place,
Every orbit had a funny face.
Cosmic jesters, bold and bright,
Brought joy to the endless night.

Celestial Serenade

In the sky, a big round face,
Wobbling, dancing in outer space.
With rings that jingle and sway,
Who knew planets could play all day?

Every moon has a quirky role,
One wears glasses, another a bowl.
They spin and twirl with such flair,
In this cosmic, silly affair.

When stars join in with a laugh,
They form a celestial photograph.
Each twinkle adds to the cheer,
A photo booth booth up here!

So here's to the fun in the night,
With planets making music so bright.
Let's dance and sing, no time to waste,
In this sky, let joy be embraced.

Moons of Melody

A moon with boots and a big guitar,
Plays tunes that echo near and far.
While others dance, they hop around,
Creating comedies, quite profound.

One moon dreams of a singing career,
Belting notes that all can hear.
But out of tune, it's more of a honk,
Causing laughter in the cosmic bonk.

With each little star, a band is formed,
Playing pranks, oh how they're warmed!
Drifting on winds of stardust dreams,
In galaxies filled with giggles and gleams.

As comets swing by with a whoosh,
The moons get up and take a swoosh.
Under the glow of a glowing sun,
They sing, they dance, oh what fun!

Harmonies in the Heavens

In the sky, a cosmic jam,
With planets sharing every slam.
They strum on rings and hum a tune,
While goofy asteroids dance to the moon.

One giant gas ball paints the scene,
Playing silly games, always seen.
While its many moons join in glee,
A musical show for all to see.

As each star flickers with delight,
They all join in, bringing pure light.
Echoes bouncing off every space,
Creating a laugh in this boundless place.

Through nebulae, the sounds take flight,
Creating memories, oh such a sight!
So let us join this merry parade,
With harmonies that won't ever fade.

The Great Gas Giant's Tune

There's a giant spinning in the sky,
With a hat made of clouds oh so shy.
It plays a tune on thunderous strings,
With melodies that joyously rings.

A band of comets gathers around,
Shouting cheers as they fly bound.
They bob their heads, quite out of sync,
As the great gas ball starts to wink.

Its massive vibe can shake the stars,
Tickling moons and even Mars.
With every laugh, the cosmos sways,
In the rhythm of the light-years' ballet.

So let the universe sing in style,
With giggles floating for miles and miles.
In the great vastness of the deep sea,
A musical giggle, joyful and free.

Atmosphere's Allure

In a dance of gas and giggles,
Where the clouds do twist and shake,
Laughter rides on swirling breezes,
As the gassy giant wakes.

Bouncing off the band of rings,
Float like balloons in the chase,
Whispers of a cosmic tune,
In this jovial, starry race.

Colors splash in vibrant pranks,
They play tag in the sky so wide,
Each twinkling star a silly wink,
As they joyously collide.

Joy bubbles in the thickened air,
Where jests are tossed like confetti,
And each gust is a cheeky laugh,
In the atmosphere all merry.

Celestial Serenades

A saxophone made of starlight,
Plays silly tunes on a whim,
Each note flutters like a moth,
In the vast, dark, cosmic gym.

Planets prance to rhymes unknown,
Bouncing round in playful glee,
With harmonies of gas and dust,
Making space a jubilee.

Across the sky, the comets dash,
With tails that sparkle and tease,
While moons chuckle, rolling by,
In rhythm with the cosmic breeze.

In this grand, galactic show,
Laughter echoes evermore,
As the universe joins in,
In a melody to explore.

Moons of Melody

Four moons twist, a merry band,
In a giggle-fueled ballet,
They leap and twirl in heady spin,
As they laugh the night away.

With faces bright and shining eyes,
They plot a prank or two,
Tickling stars with lunar beams,
In joyful, wild ado.

They serenade the cosmic night,
With rhythms of the grand unknown,
Echoing echoes from afar,
In a playful, jovial tone.

In the embrace of silvery light,
Each joke a spark, a tease,
The moons in endless revelry,
Create a symphony with ease.

Harmonics of the Giant

A giant hum fills the expanse,
In beats both quirky and bright,
Its laughter ripples through the void,
Dancing stars join in delight.

Oh, what a ruckus in the skies,
As planets get in on the play,
They wobble along with silly tunes,
In the grandest cosmic ballet.

Bubbles burst in colors bold,
Spreading joy with every sound,
Gravity's giggles roll like drums,
As the universe spins around.

With a flick and a twist, it jives,
A rollicking rhythm, no doubt,
Each pulse a riot of pure joy,
In the symphony of the stout.

Celestial Cadence

In the sky, a giant sways,
With a grin that just portrays,
Bouncing moons and swirling glee,
A dance of laughs, so wild and free.

Stars play tag, they zoom and glide,
While comets race, they slip and slide,
A cosmic giggle fills the night,
As asteroids join in the light.

Saturn's rings are hats galore,
While Mars juggles, what a score!
Cosmos laughing, twinkling bright,
Let's keep this laughter in our sight.

With each loop and silly spin,
The universe, it wears a grin,
Through laughter, planets whirl and sway,
In their own funny, cosmic play.

Vibrations of the Vast

Giggles echo in the void,
While the stardust gets employed,
Planet pals share silly jokes,
Making light of all the blokes.

Moons bounce high, such playful sights,
Tickling stars on starry nights,
Venus dances with a wink,
Who knew space could make you think?

Celestial blocks of twinkling fun,
A dance-off 'neath the glowing sun,
Gravity pulls, but who can tell,
When laughter echoes, all is well.

The rhythm's set, and off they go,
Frolicking through the cosmic show,
In vibrations bright, their tunes unite,
For space is full of pure delight.

Tuning the Starry Expanse

Stars are strumming silver strings,
Cosmic choir that laughs and sings,
In harmony, the planets play,
Making melodies every day.

Asteroids tap their tiny feet,
Comets whirl in jazzy beat,
With every note, they spin around,
Creating giggles, such a sound!

Galaxies twist in joyful cheer,
While black holes hum to bring us near,
Fun riffs bounce across the dark,
As light years dance, igniting spark.

Tuning forks of light and play,
Invite us all to join the fray,
For in this vast, delightful space,
Laughter echoes, filling the place.

Choral Waves from the Heavens

Up above, in skies so wide,
Choral waves begin to glide,
Singing songs of cosmic jest,
A symphony, they can't divest.

Nova flares throw silly hues,
While planets swap their vibrant shoes,
Neptune toots a funny tune,
As stars wink at the glowing moon.

In the void, a cosmic prank,
As space dust gathers, what a tank!
With giggles swirling through the air,
The galaxies join without a care.

A chorus of the nightly show,
With sunny laughs and moonlit glow,
Cosmic giggles, so divine,
In the realms where stars entwine.

Enigmatic Euphony

In the sky, a giant spins,
With a grin that never thins.
His moons dance in silly glee,
Twirling like kids, wild and free.

Oh, the clouds are puffs of cream,
Bouncing softly in a dream.
A whirl of color, a playful shout,
What's that ruckus? Come and scout!

Laughter bubbles in the air,
As he tricks the cosmos fair.
Stars giggle, twinkle with delight,
In the glow of the cosmic night.

So come along to this grand show,
With popcorn made from stardust, oh!
The universe plays a quirky tune,
Under the watch of the laughing moon.

Songs of the Solar Giant

A planet spins, with charm in tow,
He tickles space, and off we go!
His rings are whipped cream, fly away!
Here comes the giant's funny play.

Bouncing comets, a wild cheer,
Singing songs for all to hear.
Asteroids giggle, a merry chase,
In the big, vast, funny space.

His storms wear hats, all mismatched,
With laughter, the skies are patched.
Floating jokes in the cosmic breeze,
Whisking by like happy bees.

So join the fun, let's take a ride,
With the solar giant by our side.
In this wacky orbit, round we'll go,
Where giggles keep the night aglow.

Ethereal Echoes

There's a giant in the sky so wide,
With a heart that bursts with cosmic pride.
Echoes of laughter, sweet and bright,
Fill the heavens with sheer delight.

His storms throw confetti, oh what a sight,
As moons play marbles in the starlit night.
He juggles planets with a grin,
While all of space joins in the din.

A waltz of wonders, a merry bounce,
As stardust flutters, we can pounce!
Spinning tales of cosmic jest,
The universe joins this rambunctious fest.

In the silence of space, hear the hum,
As the giant grins, with a silly drum.
A party of planets, round and round,
In this shindig, laughter is found.

Cosmic Overture

In the center of the starry floor,
A giant winks and starts to roar.
With tunes of laughter, he sways about,
Sprinkling joy without a doubt.

His moons all drum on bubblegum,
While meteors dance, oh what a hum!
Stardust sprinkles fill the air,
As giggles bounce, a cosmic fair.

Each twinkle holds a funny tale,
As comets race, leaving a trail.
The planets whirl in silly sync,
With every beat, they start to blink.

So gather round this merry crew,
In the cosmic overture, it's true.
With laughter echoing near and far,
Join the dance beneath the stars.

Galactic Giggles

In a realm where stars wear shoes,
Dancing comets share their views.
Planets prance in silly ways,
Singing tunes on magic days.

Asteroids with wobbly grins,
Tumble down like playful twins.
Shooting stars just can't resist,
To join in laughter, join the tryst.

The space squid plays the saxophone,
As moonbeams dance, they're not alone.
Galaxies twist in sheer delight,
What a sight, oh what a sight!

Silly echoes, pop and fizzle,
As galactic giggles start to sizzle.
Every joke is light-years wide,
In this cosmic joyride!

The Atmosphere's Anthem

Clouds are puffed with giggly air,
Tickling stars that float up there.
Storms are grumpy, but they sway,
To the beat of a thunder play.

Lightning leaps like dancers free,
While the sun shines mischievously.
Rainbows laugh in colors bold,
Spinning tales that never get old.

Whirlwinds whistle silly tunes,
Nudging planets like playful loons.
Every gust brings glee anew,
Making skies a funny view!

Cosmic weather, don't you see?
Breezy jokes are the key to glee!
So let's chuckle with the stars,
And fill the void with laughter's scars!

Melodies Among the Moons

Round and round the moons will twirl,
Chasing dreams in a cosmic whirl.
Bouncing beats from cosmic paws,
Every laugh gives space applause.

Echoes dance in lunar light,
Winking stars, oh what a sight!
Moons play hopscotch, skip and yell,
In this interstellar shell.

Pluto's pals hum in a choir,
Singing songs that never tire.
Eclipses try to hide their fun,
But joy bursts forth for everyone!

In this ballet of the night,
Galactic giggles take their flight.
Melodies that loop and swirl,
Making silly dances unfurl!

Celestial Choir of Storms

A stormy choir hits the stage,
With thunder claps like a wild mage.
Raindrops tap-dance on the ground,
Such silly music all around!

Saturn's ring spins like a top,
While Jupiter's belly starts to pop.
Hurricanes hum in giddy breeze,
Whispering jokes through trees with ease.

The cosmic tympani shakes the air,
As starry giggles fill the square.
Solar flares burst with delight,
Painting skies in shades so bright!

In this whimsical stormy suite,
Who knew space could be so sweet?
Join the laugh, join the cheer,
In a universe that loves to veer!

Divinities in Orbit

In the sky, a dance so bright,
Gods on parade, what a sight!
One misplaced step, oh dear me,
Float like a feather, wild and free.

Zeus drops his thunder, what a joke,
While Venus giggles, ready to poke.
Mercury speeds, trips on his wing,
A cosmic party, let laughter ring!

Mars juggles asteroids, a daring feat,
Neptune trips over, lands on his seat.
With Saturn's rings as a playful swing,
The universe laughs, oh, what joy they bring!

In this grand theater, stars take a bow,
Galaxies whirl, take a playful vow.
Divine mischief lighting the night,
Orbiting laughter, a whimsical flight.

Cosmic Play

Planets prance in a stellar game,
Comets race, oh what a fame!
Pluto pouts, not part of the crew,
While sunlight tickles, warm and true.

Stars become marionettes, strings of light,
Twinkling away, what a whimsical sight!
Orbits collide, a friendly cheer,
As celestial children spread their glee near.

Echoes of laughter ripple through space,
Moonbeams chase the sun's bright face.
Galactic giggles paint the night sky,
In this cosmic play, spirits fly high!

Join the frolic, let your heart sway,
As the universe shouts, "Let's dance and play!"
With stars as confetti and dreams that stay,
A funny tale in this vast display.

Harmonies of Hues

In the tapestry of the night,
Colors swirl, oh what a sight!
Red, blue, and yellow join the fight,
Singing harmonies, pure delight.

Planets strum on cosmic strings,
A melody born from the laughter it brings.
With a hiccup and giggle in every note,
The universe dances, afloat and remote.

Nebulas bloom, splash of bright paint,
Auroras dance, both free and faint.
With cheers from the stars, a celestial bash,
Painting the cosmos with a vibrant splash.

So let's join in, be part of the cheer,
With laughter and colors that bring us near.
In the folds of space, let joy compose,
Harmonies of hues, where laughter flows.

Radiant Refrains

Shooting stars whistle a tune,
While moonlight twirls like a lively balloon.
Galaxies giggle, spinning around,
In this radiant choir, joy is found.

Sunbeams burst with a playful flair,
Tickling the dark with warmth to share.
Echoes of laughter bounce off the moons,
As shimmering stardust plays its tunes.

So pull up a cloud, let's sit and sway,
In this stellar concert of cosmic play.
With every refrain, we join in the fun,
A radiant moment, where we're all one.

In the vastness of night, where colors collide,
Let us sing out loud, let us not hide.
For laughter's a melody, sweet and divine,
Radiant refrains on this journey, we shine.

The Melody of the Wanderers

A giant spins in space, oh what a sight,
Dancing rings and moons, all day and night.
A storm brews wildly, a colorful show,
What's that? A cheeky comet passing below!

Silly satellites twirl in a race,
With flashes of colors, they just can't keep pace.
A waltz of the stars, they spin and they bounce,
Making up tunes that make gravity flounce!

A grand parade of planets, they all jump in line,
Hopping in rhythm, feeling just fine.
Giggles erupt as they play hide and seek,
In this cosmic carnival, oh, what a week!

So grab your space boots, let's dance on the rings,
To the whispers of the cosmos, let's see what it brings.
With laughter and whimsy, we'll twirl and we'll spin,
In the melody of wanderers, the fun never ends!

Notes from a Distant Realm

In a land far away, where the purple winds blow,
Notes of mischief and laughter start to flow.
A harp made of asteroids plays a bright tune,
While stars kick around like they're at a balloon!

Sneaky nebulae roll in with flair,
Tickling the comets as they slip through the air.
Giggles from moons, they play peekaboo,
Making the orbits wobble, oh what to do?

Planets gather 'round for a grand serenade,
Sipping on stardust, their worries will fade.
They'll chuckle and chime as they spin in delight,
Creating a symphony that dances all night!

So listen closely, hear the music arise,
From a realm that delights under twinkling skies.
With notes of enchantment and cosmic glee,
Join in this funny musical spree!

Planetary Birth

Out in the void, a planet takes shape,
With a giggle and wiggle, it starts to escape.
Gasses are swirling, with colors that pop,
From the belly of space, it's ready to hop!

Tiny rocks clink, forming rings all around,
As the planet smiles wide, it giggles out loud.
What's that? A baby star starts to sing,
And the universe dances, oh what a fling!

A funny little orbit does a silly twist,
While asteroids play tag in a cosmic mist.
With a sparkle and shine, the new world's aglow,
In the cradle of space, they steal the show!

So clap your hands for the birth of this sphere,
With laughter and light, the cosmos will cheer!
In the dance of creation, it's joy we'll unearth,
Welcome this planet, all giggles and mirth!

Cosmic Choir

Gather 'round stars, it's time for a song,
With laughter and joy, we'll all sing along.
The moon beats a drum, while planets hum low,
In the cosmic choir, we're ready to glow!

Satellites chime in with twinkling refrain,
As meteors whistle down like sweet champagne.
Orchestras of comets swipe tails high in air,
Creating a ruckus without any care!

A harmony swirls, keeps the rhythm alive,
In this space bonanza, we all start to jive.
With every bright note, the galaxies sway,
As the choir of cosmos takes center stage play!

So join in the fun, let your laughter resound,
In this orchestra vast, where mysteries abound.
With joy in our hearts and tunes in the flow,
In the cosmic choir, it's time for the show!

Symphony of the Storms

In the skies, a playful dance,
Thunder tickles, lightning prance.
Clouds wear hats, in shades so bright,
Raindrops giggle, pure delight.

Puddles jump in flirty glee,
While winds compose a silly spree.
Dancing trees in joyful cheer,
Nature's band is loud and clear.

A lightning bug hops on a beat,
Even frogs join in with their feet.
Music swells from all around,
In this storm, there's joy to be found.

As the rain taps a playful tune,
Clouds give way to a cheeky moon.
And when the sun peeks in with grin,
They all erupt and start again.

Cosmic Combustion

Stars are popping like corn in a pot,
Galaxies twirl, they give it a shot.
Planets wobble with hilarious grace,
A cosmic carnival in vast space.

The comets wear hats that swirl and twirl,
With every loop and spin, they whirl.
Meteor showers rain down confetti,
Night's a party, oh so ready!

Aliens laugh in their glowing ships,
Sharing jokes with cosmic quips.
Black holes giggle, they just can't stop,
As they munch on stardust, pop! Pop! Pop!

In this interstellar madcap play,
Celestial beings laugh all day.
Comet trails bright, a sight to behold,
In this space show, joy never gets old.

Luminous Lament

The sun spills laughter on the ground,
While shadows stretch, they dance around.
Moonbeams wink with mischievous flair,
Why do the stars tease, if they care?

Glistening lights on a sidewalk stroll,
Streetlamps giggle with a glowing role.
Happiness shines from every nook,
Even the silence has a funny hook.

Clouds drift by with stories to tell,
Each tale tickles like a charm spell.
In the gloom of night, chortles reside,
As nature's jesters take us for a ride.

As shadows fade into morning's glow,
Laughter lingers in the breezy flow.
Bright rays tickle our sleepy heads,
Making us smile as we jump from our beds.

Echoed Reverie

In echoes wide, where giggles play,
A symphony of dreams on display.
Whispers of laughter float on the air,
Tickling the night, without a care.

Reveries spin in a dance of delight,
With shadows that bounce into the night.
Chasing moonbeams, we stumble and sway,
Lost in a game where children can stay.

Every giggle ricochets from the trees,
Sparking joy like a gentle breeze.
The night is a canvas for whimsy galore,
As echoes of laughter knock on the door.

With each heartbeat, the melody blooms,
Filling the air with jubilant tunes.
In the echoing night, we dance and we sing,
In this dream of the night, we're all crowned with spring.

Harmonic Heavens

In skies so bright, the stars do laugh,
With cosmic tunes, a quirky chaff.
Planets dance in a wobbly line,
Twisting their orbits, oh so fine!

A comet sneezes, a supernova grin,
Galaxies giggle from deep within.
Asteroids roll, a playful race,
All in the name of outer space!

Silly rockets pop and fizz,
While black holes do the cha-cha whiz.
Meteor showers drop like confetti,
In a stellar party, oh so petty!

Each twinkle a wink from afar,
As planets play on a whimsical guitar.
Harmonic heavens, let the fun unfold,
In the vast universe, a tale retold!

Chorus of the Celestial Winds

The sun sings bright, a cheerful ball,
While moons spin tunes, so small and tall.
Stars wobble in a jazzy spree,
In the chorus of winds, wild and free!

Nebulas swirl, a cotton candy sight,
Twinkling in rhythms, oh what a delight!
Astro-hippos do jumping jacks,
Under the watch of cosmic tracks!

Saturn's rings twist their shiny flair,
On a merry-go-round, without a care.
Galactic grins stretch wide and far,
Each planet whistling their own bizarre!

A space-time hiccup giggles out loud,
As comets prance, gathering a crowd.
In a belt of laughter, we all align,
Singing with stars, it's truly divine!

Echoes of the Jovian Night

Oh, in the night, where shadows play,
Planets whisper silly things to say.
Moons giggle at the tales they weave,
As starlit jesters, we all believe!

A star bent forward, just to peek,
Winking at meteors on a streak.
Galaxies spin in a playful dance,
While solar winds give stars a chance!

Echoes bounce, like laughter through space,
As time takes on a carefree pace.
In cosmic fun, we lose our fright,
In the echoes of the Jovian night.

Each comet trails with a cheeky grin,
Painting the dark with a twirl and spin.
No one can resist this celestial game,
In the laughter of void, we find our fame!

Melodic Tides

With twinkling eyes, the cosmos hums,
Waves of laughter, as stardust comes.
Planets ride on melodic tides,
With whimsical waves where joy abides!

The sun plays tunes on its golden strings,
While comets join in, and friendship clings.
Galactic seas swirl in blissful flow,
As stars disco under cosmic glow!

Moons hop in rhythm, a jolly sight,
Painting the universe with sheer delight.
Astro-fish dance in stellar streams,
Chasing dreams under cosmic beams!

Melodic tides roll as laughter swells,
In a universe of merry tales.
With every wave, a giggle survives,
In the symphony where fun derives!

Ballad of the Bright Bands

In the sky, a grand parade,
With colors bursting, they invade.
The gas giant spins in a twist,
While moons dance, they can't resist.

Swirling stripes in a funky groove,
Planets pop, and the stars improve.
A cosmic tune, so light and spry,
Bringing chuckles as they fly by.

A whirlwind of laughter, it's superb,
With cosmic beans and moons that curb.
With each bounce, a grand explosion,
In this dance of cosmic motion.

So raise a cheer for the merry skies,
Where laughter lounges and fun complies.
With every turn, we join the song,
In this bright band, we all belong.

Jovial Echoes

A jovial boom from the great afar,
Echoing tunes like a twinkling star.
Galileo chuckles at the sight,
As planets giggle, oh what delight!

Bouncing balls of gas and cheer,
Flipping comets, oh so near.
Silly winds that whistle and blow,
In the vastness, playfulness flows.

Laughter swirls in a cosmic race,
A merry dance, a jovial chase.
With every swirl, a giggle rings,
The universe laughs at the joy it brings.

So listen close to the echoes bright,
In the grand expanse, pure delight.
For in this realm of galactic fun,
The music of life has just begun.

Celestial Crescendos

In the night, a playful sound,
Celestial rhythms dance around.
Stripes of color, bold and fine,
Lift the spirits, sip that wine.

The moons chuckle, the stars make light,
In the cosmic pool, there's a joyful fight.
A spiral twist, a giggle there,
In the serenade of space, we share.

Trumpets blare from the solar winds,
With every note, the laughter spins.
Galactic parties, they never cease,
With laughter blooming, filling the peace.

So join the fun in this grand ballet,
Where the skies invite us to sway.
For life is a song, a merry round,
A crescendo of joy knows no bound.

Sounds of the Shimmering Sphere

What's that sound from the twinkling sphere?
A raucous laugh, not a hint of fear.
Wobbly rings and a merry cheer,
In the cosmos, joy is ever near.

With craters that giggle and starlight winks,
The universe dances; oh, how it thinks!
Bumps and grinds of merry delight,
In the fields of stardust, we take flight.

The planets spin in a comical prance,
In this grand play, we take our chance.
A cosmic laugh track fills the air,
As worlds collide, we join the fair.

So take a moment to hear the call,
Of the shimmering sphere, we will enthrall.
For laughter echoes through the space,
In this universe, we find our place.

Whims of the Gas Giant

In swirling hues of orange and blue,
A giant laughs, what a sight to view.
He spins and twirls, like a playful kite,
Chasing his moons in the velvet night.

With a thunderous giggle, he shakes the stars,
Bouncing his clouds like bumpy guitars.
With each gusty breeze, he tickles the skies,
All the little planets look up with surprise.

Oh, what a character with storms so grand,
His hurricane dances, a reckless band.
When he rolls his eyes, comets zip by,
Waving to all in the cosmic sky.

Round and round, he makes his way,
Donning a crown of gas, oh so gay.
Cheerful and chubby, with a smile so wide,
His laughter echoes through the galactic ride.

Harmonious Roll

A big ol' ball in a game of space,
He twirls around with an endless grace.
The moons chuckle softly, they roll along,
Joining in sunbeams, they hum a song.

Bouncing and swirling, a jovial sight,
He tickles the rings with all of his might.
The asteroids giggle, they skip to the beat,
As the cosmic band makes their tune complete.

Wobbling gently, the giant takes charge,
His tempestuous laughter, dangerously large.
Each gassy puff puffs out a tune,
Filling the cosmos with a quirky croon.

In this dance of wonder, all stains are erased,
As joy and brightness encompass the space.
He launches his jest with each playful spin,
Planetary parties always begin!

Artistry of the Infinite

With swirls of pastel, the gas giant plays,
Painting soft dreams in vibrant arrays.
His artistry sparkles, a canvas of air,
Masterpiece whimsy floating with flair.

Clouds form critters, that grin and strut,
Bouncing together, they giggle and cut.
With each twist and turn, the colors delight,
Adventures in laughter, they dance through the night.

Will-o'-the-wisps chase across his face,
Bubbling with joy in an endless embrace.
Through storms of hilarity, comets drift past,
Creating a show that will always last.

The lessons of laughter are written in space,
Each jovial swirl leaves a cheeky trace.
In the grand art gallery of the vast night,
His playful demeanor reflects pure delight.

Celestial Ballet

In the vast ballroom of cosmic delight,
He frolics and whirls, a bewildering sight.
Dressed in gas robes that puff and sway,
A partners' charade in the Milky Way.

His moons pirouette with a gleeful cheer,
As laughter erupts through the atmosphere.
The stars join the dance with a twinkling glance,
Creating a waltz that invites every chance.

With each graceful turn, he bows to the void,
His stormy encore, wonderfully enjoyed.
As meteors shimmy and asteroids spin,
They all join the fun with a cheeky grin.

In this galactic dance, all troubles dissolve,
Each movement a riddle that stars must resolve.
A ballet of whimsy, in galaxies far,
The giant twirls brightly, our cosmic star.

Solar Serenades

In space so vast, a dance begins,
With little moons and playful spins.
A comet sneezes, what a sight,
Stars giggle in the velvet night.

A meteor slides with a wink and twirl,
Grinning softly, it gives a whirl.
Planets chuckle in a cosmic race,
While asteroids laugh, a raucous chase.

The sun beams down with a hearty cheer,
Sunglasses on, it's bright here, my dear!
So let's take flight on this merry ride,
In the grand galactic joy we'll glide.

Between the orbits, jokes take flight,
Galaxies spin with all their might.
Each twinkling star, a joke untold,
In this solar dance, we feel the bold.

Rhythm of the Cosmic Tide

Celestial waves roll in with a laugh,
Nebulas swirl in a cosmic bath.
Shooting stars taking silly spills,
As laughter echoes through space's hills.

The moons play tag in a celestial game,
While the sun throws shade, and nobody's to blame.
Asteroids giggle as they pass by,
Tickling comets, oh me, oh my!

Twinkling lights make a big parade,
Space cows jump in, a cosmic charade.
Galactic winds whistle a tune,
As planets spin under a silly moon.

With every orbit, the laughter grows,
A dance of joy where the fun just flows.
Join the rhythm, let your spirit soar,
In this vast expanse, there's so much more!

Voices of the Ether

In the ether, whispers make us grin,
Galactic gossip where nonsense begins.
Stars are chattering, "Did you hear?,"
While rainbow comets float without fear.

A gas giant giggles, puffing out air,
"Who wore it better?" it does declare.
While satellites spin in a social swirl,
Exchanging tales, a cosmic whirl.

Constellations roll their twinkling eyes,
As black holes smirk with mysterious sighs.
In this laughter, there's joy to find,
Voices of the ether, oh, how they bind!

With every echo, humor transcends,
In the void, the laughter never ends.
So come and join this whimsical flight,
Where the stars are bright and spirits ignite!

Melodies of the Majestic

In the realm where the music sways,
Planets hum in harmonious ways.
Each note a giggle, each chord a cheer,
In the symphony of space, gather near!

A supernova blooms, so bright and loud,
While stardust dances in a lively crowd.
The moon cracks jokes with a silver tone,
As fiery suns play with light of their own.

Galaxies spin in a swirling delight,
With cosmic rhythms in the depth of night.
A tune drifts softly on the solar breeze,
While gravity's pull draws us to our knees.

So let's raise a cheer for this funny show,
In the vast expanse where giggles flow.
Melodies weave through the starry skies,
In this cosmic concert, joy never dies!

Nighttime Nocturne

In the sky, a giant bound,
Rolling in with goofy sounds.
His moons dance in a silly spree,
Wobbling like they're on a spree.

Bouncing off the starry stage,
He writes jokes upon the page.
Galactic gales of laughter burst,
In cosmic comedy, we trust.

With a grin, he pulls a prank,
Filling space with goofy yanks.
While aliens chuckle, hide, and peek,
All are joyous, none feel weak.

Under velvet dark, they play,
Silly stars perform all day.
Galactic giggles never cease,
In this night of purest peace.

Cosmic Crescendo

A joker on a swirling throne,
Twirling puns like cosmic foam.
Each moon a buddy, here to play,
Making comet trails sway.

With each bounce, a chuckle grows,
Infusing space with funny flows.
Planets join in merry cheer,
Echoing laughter across the sphere.

Starry laughter fills the void,
In the cosmos, no one's coy.
Floats a grin on every face,
In this light years of embrace.

Rockets zoom from here to there,
Spreading jokes through stellar air.
A universe of pure delight,
Where humor shines through every night.

Lunar Lullabies

Twinkling stars hum soft and bright,
Whispering fun in the moonlight.
Planets sway, all in a row,
Humming tunes that ebb and flow.

The craters giggle, side by side,
Where shadows play and dreams reside.
A cosmic choir sings in glee,
Lullabies that tickle me.

Full moons wink with cheeky grace,
Jokes exchanged in quiet space.
As solar winds gently tease,
Stars erupt in belly laughs, at ease.

In this realm where humor sways,
All our cares are cast away.
With every note, a joyful sigh,
In the night where fairies fly.

Whispers of the Thunder King

A giant cloaked in stormy jest,
With thunderous laughter, he's the best.
Mighty storms that rumble low,
Share silly secrets in their flow.

His lightning flickers, dances bright,
Making shadows leap with fright.
Yet in the roar, there lies a grin,
As storms and stars begin to spin.

Galactic giggles grace the skies,
While meteors howl and angels rise.
Each roar a punchline, neat and sweet,
Rolling laughter beneath his feet.

From high above, he casts his cheer,
To every creature far and near.
In the whispers of the night,
Lies the king of cosmic light.

Moons in Orbit

Round and round they spin and sway,
Chasing light both night and day.
One's a clown, the other's shy,
Twisting tales when they fly by.

Poking fun at each bright star,
These little moons get quite bizarre.
Jumping high, then falling low,
In their dance, they steal the show.

With a wink and secret grin,
They know the night is where to win.
A leap, a twirl, a silly hop,
Around the planet they won't stop!

Laughter echoing through the night,
In their orbits, pure delight.
Oh what fun, what crazy sights,
The moons play games of silly flights.

Starlit Reveries

Stars giggle in the velvet sea,
Whispering dreams and jubilee.
A twinkle here, a wink from there,
They play tag in cosmic air.

Puffed up clouds of fluffy white,
Join the fun, a pure delight.
Chasing comets, racing light,
Underneath the moon so bright.

Cosmic pranks with meteors,
Throwing sparkles, open doors.
Galaxies spin, in starlit glee,
As laughter echoes endlessly.

Each flicker tells a cheeky tale,
In the endless, swirling trail.
With every giggle, every cheer,
The universe feels oh so near.

Celestial Rhapsody

Planets pirouette with flair,
In a dance that fills the air.
Silly rhythms, cosmic tunes,
Bouncing bright among the moons.

Laughter erupts from deep space,
As stars attempt a dance-off race.
With every spin, a star goes pop,
They giggle on, they never stop!

Shooting stars that freely dash,
Make a wish, but then they crash.
Playful sparks in a savory stew,
Celestial quirks for me and you.

In this rhapsody of light,
Even shadows feel the bright.
Round and round, we can't resist,
The universe's joyful twist!

Astral Accompaniment

A comet waves, a wink so sly,
Shooting quickly through the sky.
Planets hum a merry tune,
While asteroids play hide-and-seek, with a spoon.

In the dark, they form a band,
Playing rhythms, oh so grand.
A galactic giggle, cosmic beat,
Is it music, or just their feet?

Nebulas spark like silly lights,
Creating joy in starry nights.
They strum on stars with such delight,
In this dance, they're feeling bright.

Every twirl, a note to share,
With laughter weaving through the air.
So come and join this astral show,
Where fun and stars continually flow.

Harmonies Beyond the Horizon

In a land where balloons float,
Laughter comes from a silly goat.
Dancing stars with hats so bright,
Giggles echo through the night.

Bouncing beans on trampoline,
Wobbling jelly, what a scene!
Tickle fights with cosmic rays,
Eclipsing worries in funny ways.

Singing whales with rubber bands,
Ticklish toes in far-off lands.
Juggling meteors, what a sight,
Stars drink soda, oh what a night!

Space mice tap-dance on the moon,
A serenade to a silly tune.
With each laugh, the cosmos sways,
Join the fun, let's laugh for days!

Serenades of the Spheres

Round and round the planets spin,
With monkey hats and cheeky grins.
Giggly stars in limousines,
Holding hands in vibrant scenes.

Silly sounds from outer space,
Aliens in a wild chase.
Marshmallow comets zoom and glide,
While candy clouds do the moonwalk slide.

Bouncing balls of glittery jam,
Banana ships sail with a slam.
Singing cats with bow ties swing,
To the rhythm of a cosmic fling.

Spinning tops on astral stage,
Every rock has its own page.
Cackling laughs from twinkling foes,
Let's dance along, as the universe glows!

Aetherial Orchestrations

Up above, where the turtles fly,
Juggling planets as they sigh.
Bubbling streams of fizzy cheer,
Streamers float, the party's here.

Whimsical wands create a show,
Sparklers twirl in gleeful flow.
Cosmic kites dance in the wind,
Mirthful tunes that never end.

Sassy squirrels with flutes in hand,
Sing to planets, a merry band.
With every note, the starlight glows,
The laughter spreads; oh, how it goes!

A whirl of colors fills the sky,
While each ticklish breeze floats by.
Join the laughter, don't delay,
Let's orbit joy in a playful way!

Alien Anthems

Martian frogs with bright pink hats,
Jumping high like playful cats.
Laughter bursts in every tune,
As rockets dance beneath the moon.

Bouncing stars with silly masks,
Ask the comet; it's no task.
Gumbo in a sizzling pan,
Wobbling like a wobbly man.

Singing blobs from distant lands,
Share their jokes with flailing hands.
Galactic giggles fill the night,
Where aliens laugh with pure delight.

Dancing loons with ice cream cones,
Make stardust dreams from silly tones.
Join this cosmic, funny plight,
For laughter sparkles, pure and bright!

Orbiting Odes

A giant's dance in endless space,
With swirling rings that spin with grace.
He wears a crown of stormy glee,
While moons play tag—oh, what a spree!

His laughter echoes, bold and bright,
A cosmic joke that feels just right.
The stars are clapping, lights aglow,
As tiny comets steal the show.

With twinkling eyes, they spin and zoom,
Around the king, they make their room.
A playground set on velvet night,
Where every bounce brings pure delight!

So come and join this jolly ride,
Where jovial pranks cannot be denied.
As satellites spin with a cheer,
And giggles travel far and near!

A Chorus of Cloudscapes

Up high, the fluffy marshmallows play,
They toss and tumble in a grand ballet.
With sunlit glimmers all around,
They whisper secrets, laughter bound!

A choir formed of vapors bright,
Sings silly songs that tickle light.
Each puff a joke, each wisp a grin,
In this soft realm where fun begins.

They drift away on breezy trails,
Carrying tales of windy gales.
With every giggle, clouds collide,
In this vast space where joys abide.

So lift your gaze and catch the cheer,
Join in the fun; the sky's sincere.
As breezes dance and giggles whir,
Come share the clouds - let laughter stir!

Echoes of the Thunder God

In the distance roars a grand surprise,
A jolly thunder that shakes the skies.
With booming laughter, the storm clouds play,
Sparkling bolts dance in a wild display.

The trickster laughs with booming might,
Flashing bright, day turns to night.
As raindrops fall like giggles light,
Each splash a chuckle, pure delight!

Around and around, the echoes clash,
With hearty bellows, it starts to splash.
Lightning wiggles, twirls with glee,
A funny show for you and me.

So hold onto hats, don't fly away,
As the sky jests in its playful way.
Join in the frolic, let voices soar,
In the thunder's smile, we find much more!

Skylit Soundscapes

Beneath the canvas of twinkling night,
Frolicsome stars twirl, glowing bright.
They dance to tunes that galaxies hum,
As space whispers softly, 'Here they come!'

With every wink, they toss a jest,
A sprinkle of joy - oh, isn't it best?
Cosmic giggles echo afar,
As laughter weaves through each twinkling star.

The moon joins in with a cheeky grin,
In this sky party, let the fun begin!
As comets race, chasing after dreams,
The universe chuckles, bursting at the seams.

So catch this rhythm, join the play,
In the soundscape where silliness stays.
With cosmic sounds, let worries cease,
In these bright moments, find your peace!

Cosmic Cadence

In the vast night, a twinkle takes flight,
A mischievous star with a smile so bright.
It jiggles and dances, oh, what a sight,
Bouncing through space, it's pure delight.

Planets all chuckle, they join in the play,
As comets come whizzing, whoosh, hooray!
With laughter and giggles, they light up the way,
In this cosmic ballet, it's a rollicking day.

Asteroids wobbly, with hats made of cheese,
Spin round and round in a whimsical breeze.
Twirling like children, as light as you please,
In the dance of the cosmos, it's sure to tease.

So fellow stargazers, come take a glance,
At the radiant jesters, taking their chance.
In the vast cosmic hall, they lead the romance,
With a wink and a giggle, they twirl in their dance.

Tales from the Red Spot

In the swirling storm where giggles reside,
A big, blustery fellow drifts with great pride.
He tells all the planets, come take a ride,
In his whirlwind fun, there's nothing to hide.

He spins out tall tales of laughter and cheer,
With clouds made of candy that drift ever near.
Each whisper a chuckle that all love to hear,
In the storm's joyful grasp, there's naught left to fear.

Around him they gather, those curious sprites,
Fetching stardust and laughter on whimsical nights.
They play peekaboo games, avoiding his bites,
As he chuckles and rumbles, igniting the lights.

So next time you gaze at the great swirling spot,
Remember the stories are funny a lot.
In this jolly domain, they comically trot,
With giggles galore, in the cosmos, we've got!

Starlit Serenade

Under a blanket of shimmering space,
Stars sing a tune with a giggly grace.
They twirl through the night, a playful embrace,
In a melody bright, they set the pace.

The moon joins the chorus, with laughter so sweet,
As planets all tap to the rhythm of beat.
With meteors dashing, they can't find their seat,
In this starlit affair, it's a whimsical feat.

Galaxies rolling in tunes of delight,
While space dust sparkles, it's a comical sight.
The universe chuckles, all through the night,
With laughter and joy, oh what pure light!

So let the stars guide you, don't miss the fun,
As they bounce and they wiggle, the party's begun.
In the cosmic arena, under the sun,
Tune into the mirth, where laughter is spun.

Stratosphere Soundtrack

High in the sky, where the giggles reside,
A jive of the clouds in a comical glide.
With breezes of laughter, they bounce and they bide,
In a symphony bright, there's joy to confide.

Wind instruments whistle, trees hum along,
A tune made of giggles, a jolly old song.
While rainbows keep dancing, where they all belong,
In the stratosphere's arms, celebrations are strong.

So take to the air with a skip and a hop,
Join the fluttering notes that just never stop.
With echoes of chuckles, let worries just drop,
In this jazzy parade, happiness will pop!

With every soft gust, there's a sprinkle of cheer,
In the vast open skies, let your laughter draw near.
So float with the clouds, let go of your fear,
In this stratosphere journey, life's funny and clear!

www.ingramcontent.com/pod-product-compliance
Lightning Source LLC
Chambersburg PA
CBHW072214070526
44585CB00015B/1328